Credit Union Merger and Conversion Manual

NCUA 8056/M 6300

TABLE OF CONTENTS

Topic *Page*

INTRODUCTION 3

CHAPTER 1 - MERGERS

STEP 1: DO SOME EARLY THINKING
- Permissibility of the Merger 4
- Analysis of Probable Asset/Share Ratio 6
- Accounting Implications of the Merger 7
- Other Board of Directors Considerations 7

STEP 2: PREPARE AND SUBMIT THE MERGER PACKAGE
- Contents of the Merger Package 8
- Items Specific to Corporate Credit Unions 9
- Tips to Speed Up the Approval Process 10
- NCUA Approval 10

STEP 3: CONDUCT THE MEMBERSHIP VOTE
- Member Notification 11
- Votes Needed for Approval 12

STEP 4: COMPLETE THE MERGER
- Federal Share Insurance Coverage 12
- Federal Trade Commission Notification 14
- Surety Bond Coverage 14
- Required Forms 15
- Charter Cancellation 15

CHAPTER 2 – CONVERTING TO PRIVATE INSURANCE

STEP 1: PREPARE FOR THE CONVERSION
- Permissibility of the Conversion 16
- Notify NCUA 16

STEP 2: CONDUCT THE MEMBERSHIP VOTE
- Member Notification 16
- Communicating With Your Members 17
- Vote Requirements 17

STEP 3: COMPLETE THE CONVERSION
- Federal Share Insurance Coverage 18
- Required Certification 18

GLOSSARY OF TERMS 19

APPENDIX A - MERGER FORMS

APPENDIX B – INSURANCE CONVERSION FORMS

INTRODUCTION

This Credit Union Merger and Conversion Manual (Manual) provides guidance and forms for credit unions planning to merge with other credit unions or planning to convert from federal share insurance to private share insurance. The Manual replaces previously issued Credit Union Merger Manuals.

This Manual covers mergers and conversions involving both federal and state chartered credit unions and corporate credit unions. It summarizes portions of the following regulations:

- Mergers of Federally-Insured Credit Unions; Voluntary Termination or Conversion of Insured Status, Part 708b of NCUA's Rules and Regulations.

- Chartering and Field of Membership Manual, NCUA Interpretive Ruling and Policy Statement (IRPS) 03-1.

Credit unions should refer to the full text of Part 708b or IRPS 03-1 as needed for additional information. Both regulations are available on NCUA's website: www.ncua.gov.

Converting credit unions needing additional assistance may contact their State Supervisory Authority or NCUA Regional Office. Credit unions should consult with legal and accounting professionals as necessary to plan and execute a merger or conversion properly.

CHAPTER 1 - MERGERS

STEP 1: DO SOME EARLY THINKING

Permissibility of the Merger

Part 708b of the National Credit Union Administration's (NCUA) Rules and Regulations describes our procedures and notice requirements for mergers involving a federally insured credit union:

- If the continuing credit union is a federal credit union (FCU), the merger must follow NCUA's chartering policies.

- If the continuing and/or merging credit unions are state-chartered, prior approval of the appropriate state regulator(s) must be obtained, and any applicable state regulations must be followed. In addition, NCUA's field of membership policies do not apply.

- If a federally insured credit union merges into a nonfederally insured (privately insured) or uninsured state-chartered credit union, the merger must follow state laws and federal laws related to share insurance conversion or termination.

A federally-insured credit union must have the prior written approval of the NCUA before merging with any other credit union.

The following is a synopsis of the permissibility of different types of mergers. For more detailed information, federal credit unions should see NCUA's Chartering and Field of Membership Manual (IRPS 03-1).

Scenario 1: The continuing credit union is state-chartered
The merger is permissible if—
- State requirements are followed.

While NCUA's field of membership policies do not apply when the continuing credit union is state-chartered, a merging *federal* credit union must follow NCUA's voting requirements.

Scenario 2: A single common bond CU merging into another single common bond FCU
The merger is permissible if—
- Both CUs share a common bond; or
- It is an emergency merger (see scenario 9).

Scenario 3: Multiple common bond CU merging into a multiple common bond FCU
The merger is permissible if—
- Each select group in the merging credit union's field of membership has fewer than 3,000 primary potential members; or
- It is a supervisory or emergency merger (see scenario 8 or 9).

If any select group in the merging credit union's field of membership has 3,000 or more primary potential members, and the continuing credit union does not serve the group, NCUA must analyze the group to determine whether the group could form its own credit union, unless it is a supervisory or emergency merger (see scenario 8 or 9).

Scenario 4: Single common bond CU with a primary potential membership less than 3,000, merging into a multiple common bond FCU
The merger is permissible.

Scenario 5: Single common bond CU with a primary potential membership of 3,000 or more, merging into a multiple common bond FCU
The merger is permissible if—
- The continuing credit union already has within its field of membership the group served by the merging single common bond FCU; or
- It is an emergency merger (see scenario 9).

Scenario 6: A single or multiple common bond CU merging into a community chartered FCU
The merger is permissible if—
- The merging credit union has a service facility within the community boundaries;
- A majority of the merging credit union's field of membership would qualify for membership in the community chartered federal credit union;
- The continuing community chartered FCU previously added an underserved area and the merging credit union's field of membership is contained within the specific underserved area; or
- It is an emergency merger (see scenario 9).

Groups within the merging credit union's field of membership located outside the community boundaries of the continuing FCU may not continue to be served. However, the credit union can continue to serve members of record. If the merging CU is state-chartered, the approval of the state regulators is required.

Scenario 7: Community chartered CU merging into a community chartered FCU
The merger is permissible if—
- The merging CU's boundaries are entirely within the continuing FCU's boundaries;
- The continuing FCU meets the criteria for expanding its boundaries to include the merging CU's boundaries;
- a majority of the merging credit union's field of membership would qualify for membership in the community chartered FCU; or
- It is an emergency merger (see scenario 9).

Scenario 8: Supervisory merger (only applies to multiple common bond credit unions)
The merger is permissible if supervisory concerns exist. That is, the merging credit union is experiencing safety and soundness concerns. Examples of these concerns include; abandonment of management and/or officials and an inability to find replacements, loss of sponsor support, serious and persistent recordkeeping problems, sustained material decline in financial condition, or other serious or persistent circumstances.

We can act on supervisory merger applications without regard to the 3,000 numerical limitation and the merging credit union does not need to be insolvent or in danger of insolvency.

Scenario 9: Emergency merger
The merger is permissible if an emergency exists. That is, the merging credit union is insolvent or likely to become insolvent. A few conditions that may lead to insolvency: abandonment by management, loss of sponsor, or serious and persistent record keeping problems.

We can act on emergency merger applications without regard to field of membership requirements, the 3,000 numerical limitation or other legal constraints. However, we must determine (a) an emergency exists, (b) other alternatives are not reasonably available, and (c) the public interest will best be served by approving the merger.

Scenario 10: Corporate credit unions
The merger is permissible if deemed to be in the best interest of the corporate credit union's natural person credit union members. In cases where the continuing and/or merging corporate credit unions are state-chartered, the prior approval of the appropriate state regulator(s) must be obtained, and any applicable state regulations must be followed.

Analysis of Probable Asset/Share Ratio

As part of the merger plan, a share analysis is required for both the merging and continuing credit unions. To help you with the share analysis, you can use Forms NCUA 6311 and 6312 in Appendix A or download the spreadsheets from our web site at www.ncua.gov.

The probable asset/share ratio (PAS) is the relative worth of each $1 in shares, assuming the credit union is an ongoing concern. The PAS can be used as a tool to determine whether a merging dividend is appropriate.

The PAS is not applicable to corporate credit unions. As such, corporate credit unions need not submit Forms NCUA 6311 and 6312 as part of their merger package. In lieu of the PAS calculation, corporate credit unions should provide a schedule of the retained earnings, core capital, and capital ratios as set forth in Part 704 of NCUA's Rules and Regulations. The ratios are to be calculated for the merging and continuing corporates, as well as on a consolidated basis.

Accounting Implications of the Merger

Section 741.6 of NCUA's Rules and Regulations requires that all insured credit unions file quarterly call reports. Credit unions with assets of $10 million or greater must follow generally accepted accounting principles (GAAP). The Financial Accounting Standards Board requires the purchase accounting method for business combinations generally, but has granted a deferral of the effective date for the application of purchase accounting to the merger of mutual enterprises, i.e., merger of a credit union with another credit union. During the period of this deferral, credit unions may continue to simply combine (add together) the financial statement components of the two merging credit unions.

Credit unions planning to merge should obtain the advice of a qualified accountant on the accounting implications of the planned merger.

Other Board of Directors Considerations

Before you vote to merge with another credit union, you should notify your NCUA District Examiner and consider the following:

- Alternatives to merging, such as working with a mentor credit union or expanding your credit union's field of membership.

- The potential impact on your credit union's financial condition and operational capacity to serve the combined membership.

- Whether the merger is in your members' best interest.

After you vote, you should complete Form NCUA 6302 or 6303 in Appendix A, as appropriate.

STEP 2: PREPARE AND SUBMIT THE MERGER PACKAGE

Contents of the Merger Package

The continuing credit union completes the merger package. Check to see that your package is complete by using Form NCUA 6301, Merger Package Checklist, in Appendix A.

1. Details required for **all** merger packages:

    - Detailed explanation of the reason for the merger.
    - Proposed effective date of the merger.
    - Current financial statements (same reporting period) for both credit unions.
    - Current delinquent loan summary (same reporting period) for both credit unions.
    - Current analysis of the adequacy of the Allowance for Loan and Lease Losses Account (same reporting period) for both credit unions.
    - Consolidated financial statements, including an assessment of net worth of each credit union before the merger and the net worth of the continuing credit union after the merger.
    - Analyses of share values (Forms NCUA 6311 and 6312 in Appendix A). This requirement is not applicable to corporate credit unions. In lieu of Forms NCUA 6311 and 6312, corporate credit unions are to submit a schedule of the retained earnings, core capital, and capital ratios as set forth in Part 704 of NCUA's Rules and Regulations. The ratios are to be calculated for the merging and continuing corporates, as well as on a consolidated basis.
    - Explanation of any proposed share adjustment.
    - Proposed Merger Agreement (Form NCUA 6304 in Appendix A) stating any terms related to share adjustments. **This copy must not be dated, signed, or notarized at this time.** Submit the executed final merger agreement only after the merger is approved and completed.
    - Explanation of any provisions for reserves, undivided earnings, or dividends.
    - Provisions for notifying and paying creditors.
    - Explanation of any changes to insurance, such as life savings and insurance of member accounts.
    - Copies of the fields of membership for the merging and continuing credit unions.
    - Information on where the members will be served. Include the location of the continuing credit union office(s) and whether there are plans to serve the members through the merging credit union's existing office(s).
    - If the merging credit union has $50 million or more in assets on its latest call report, a statement about whether the two credit unions intend to make a Hart-Scott-Rodino Act (HSRA) premerger notification filing with the Federal Trade Commission and, if not, why not (see Page 14).

- One primary contact person at both the merging and continuing credit unions. Include their mailing addresses, e-mail addresses, and phone numbers (for questions or notification of merger decisions).
- Resolutions of both boards of directors (Forms NCUA 6302 and 6303 in Appendix A).
- From the merging federal credit union, a proposed Notice of Special Meeting of the Members (Form NCUA 6305A, 6305B, or 6305C in Appendix A). **We can waive the vote by members of the merging federal credit union only if the merging credit union is insolvent or in danger of insolvency and is merging into another federally insured credit union.**
- From the merging federal credit union, a copy of the ballot to be sent to the members (Form NCUA 6306A, 6306B, or 6306C in Appendix A).

2. Details required of **some** merger packages:

- If the merging credit union is state-chartered and the continuing credit union is federally chartered, provisions for determining that all assets and liabilities of the continuing credit union will conform with the Federal Credit Union Act.
- If applicable, evidence your State Supervisory Authority approves of the proposed merger.
- If the continuing credit union is not federally-insured and will not apply for federal insurance, (a) a written statement from the continuing credit union that it is aware of the requirements of 12 U.S.C. §1831t(b), including all notification and acknowledgment requirements and (b) proof that the accounts of the merging credit union will be accepted for coverage by the nonfederal insurer (private insurer).

Items Specific to Corporate Credit Unions

In addition to the items required of natural person credit union merger packages in #1 and #2 above, a corporate credit union must also include a merger consolidation plan which addresses the following areas:

- Budget,
- Strategic plan,
- Marketing,
- Capital accumulation, and
- Information systems conversion and integration.

Corporate credit union examiners will perform on-site and off-site analyses of merger packages prior to official action being taken on the request. Examiners will meet with senior management to:

- Review the merger plan documents,
- Ensure an appropriate staff person has been assigned overall responsibility for supervising the merger process, and
- Determine whether a retention and contingency plan for key employees has been established.

The examiners will review the continuing corporate's plans for each department, operational area, and/or branch facility, as well as meet with key personnel in each area, to determine whether:

- Staffing and technology needs are adequately addressed,
- Overhead costs have been analyzed and allocated,
- Task lists and time tables are reasonable,
- Plans are in place to communicate necessary information to the members of the merging corporate,
- Contingency plans have been developed to address any problems as they emerge; and
- Reporting mechanisms are in place to ensure senior management and the board of directors are informed of the merger's progress.

Tips to Speed Up the Approval Process

You can speed up the merger process in two ways:

- Notify NCUA and, if applicable, your State Supervisory Authority as early as possible of your intent to merge.

- Simultaneously provide a complete merger package to both NCUA and, if applicable, your State Supervisory Authority.

NCUA Approval

NCUA will approve the proposed merger if the merger:

- Is in the best interest of the members;
- Meets the requirements of the Federal Credit Union Act, NCUA's Rules and Regulations, and IRPS 03-1;
- Minimizes undue risk to the NCUSIF; and
- Meets applicable state law, as determined by the State Supervisory Authority.

If the NCUA Regional Director denies the proposed merger, he or she will provide you with an explanation for the denial and your right to appeal the decision. After the denial, you have 30 days to provide supplemental information for the regional director's reconsideration or 60 days to appeal the decision to the NCUA Board.

Only the NCUA Board has the authority to approve corporate credit union mergers. Merger requests are to be submitted to the Director of the Office of Corporate Credit Unions (OCCU). The OCCU Director will submit the merger proposal to the NCUA Board for appropriate action. Corporate credit unions are encouraged to contact OCCU early in the merger process for any additional information and guidance.

STEP 3: CONDUCT THE MEMBERSHIP VOTE

Member Notification

After NCUA approves your merger proposal, the merging federal credit union must present the proposal for approval at a membership meeting. Members have the right to vote on the merger proposal.

- In person at the annual meeting (if it takes place within 60 days after NCUA approval),
- At a special meeting to be called within 60 days of NCUA approval, or
- By mail or electronic ballot received no later than the date and time announced for the annual meeting or the special meeting called for that purpose.

You are also required to give members of the merging federal credit union advance notice of the meeting. You must mail or deliver the notice and ballot in person to each member at least 7 days before the scheduled meeting. The notice should include the following:

- The purpose, time, and location of the meeting.
- A summary of the merger plan, including individual and consolidated financial statements for the two credit unions.
- Reasons for the proposed merger.
- The name and location of the continuing credit union.
- The members have the right to vote on the merger proposal in person at the meeting, or by written ballot to be received no later than the date and time announced for the meeting.
- A copy of the merger proposal ballot.

Merging federally-insured state chartered credit unions must follow state requirements.

Votes Needed for Approval

<u>Scenario 1: FCU merging into a federally insured credit union</u>
A majority of the members of the merging credit union who vote on the proposal must approve the merger.

<u>Scenario 2. FCU merging into an uninsured credit union</u>
A majority of the merging credit union's total membership must approve the merger and termination of insurance. An independent entity must collect and tally the votes and certify the results. The vote must be taken by secret ballot, meaning that no credit union employee or official can determine how a particular member voted.

<u>Scenario 3: FCU merging into a nonfederally insured (privately insured) credit union</u>
A majority of the merging credit union's members who vote on the proposal must approve the merger and insurance conversion, provided at least 20 percent of the total membership participates in the voting. An independent entity must collect and tally the votes and certify the results. The vote must be taken by secret ballot, meaning that no credit union employee or official can determine how a particular member voted.

With all three scenarios, mail and electronic ballots must be received no later than the date and time announced for the membership meeting.

<u>Merging federally-insured state chartered credit unions must follow state requirements.</u>

STEP 4: COMPLETE THE MERGER

Federal Share Insurance Coverage

Part 708b.101 of NCUA's Rules and Regulations describes the special provisions for federal share insurance coverage in merger situations.

<u>Scenario 1: Continuing credit union is federally insured</u>
NCUA will assess a National Credit Union Share Insurance Fund (NCUSIF) capitalization deposit based on insured share dollars if the merging credit union is a nonfederally insured (privately insured) or uninsured credit union. While historically rare, an insurance premium may be assessed for all federally insured credit unions during the calendar year. If a premium is assessed in the year the merger takes place, a prorated insurance premium on the additional share accounts insured as a result of the merger will be charged.

If both the merging and continuing credit unions are federally-insured and the two credit unions have overlapping fields of membership, the continuing credit union must, within three months after completion of the merger, either: (a) notify all members of the continuing credit union of the potential loss of insurance coverage if they had overlapping membership, (b) notify all individuals and entities that were actually members of both credit unions of the potential loss of insurance coverage, or (c) determine which members of both credit unions may actually have uninsured funds six months after the merger and notify those members of the potential loss of insurance coverage.

Scenario 2: Continuing credit union wants to convert to federal insurance
When the continuing credit union is nonfederally insured (privately insured) or uninsured but wants to be federally insured, the credit union needs to submit an application for federal insurance to the appropriate NCUA Regional Director at least 90 days before the merger application. If we approve the insurance application, then we will assess a NCUSIF capitalization deposit based on insured share dollars. While historically rare, an insurance premium may be assessed for all federally insured credit unions during the calendar year. If a premium is assessed in the year the merger takes place, a prorated insurance premium on the additional share accounts insured as a result of the merger will be charged.

Scenario 3: Continuing credit union is uninsured, but the merging credit union is federally insured
After the one-year period of continued insurance coverage, we will provide the continuing credit union with a refund of the merging credit union's NCUSIF capitalization deposit and a refund of any unused portion of the NCUSIF share insurance premium if one was assessed in the year the merger took place.

The merging, federally insured credit union must notify its members of the discontinuance of federal insurance before they vote on the proposed merger (Form NCUA 6305C in Appendix A).

Scenario 4: Continuing credit union is nonfederally insured (privately insured), but the merging credit union is federally insured
NCUSIF insurance of the member accounts of the merging credit union ceases as of the effective date of the merger. The merging federally insured credit union must notify its members of the discontinuance of federal insurance before they vote on the proposed merger (Form NCUA 6305B in Appendix A).

Under both Scenarios 3 and 4 where the continuing credit union is not federally-insured, the continuing credit union must submit the following:

- A written statement that it is aware of the requirements of 12 U.S.C. §1831t(b), including all notification and acknowledgment requirements; and
- Proof that the accounts of the credit union will be accepted for coverage by the nonfederal insurer (private insurer) (in the case of Scenario 4).

Federal Trade Commission Notification

Under the Hart-Scott-Rodino Antitrust Improvements Act of 1976 (HSRA), as amended, some merging credit unions must submit prior notification of the merger to the Federal Trade Commission (FTC). The purpose of the filing is to give the FTC an opportunity to review the proposed merger to determine if it would violate federal antitrust laws. If the merging credit union reported more than $50 million in assets on its last call report, your merger proposal must state whether you plan to make a HSRA filing and if not, why not.

For more information, see the FTC's web site at www.ftc.gov.

Surety Bond Coverage

The continuing federal credit union needs to review its surety bond coverage to ensure compliance with Part 713 of NCUA's Rules and Regulations. The continuing federal credit union must have the minimum dollar amount of coverage as of the effective date of the merger. It also should notify its surety bond carrier of a pending merger.

The merging credit union cannot cancel its surety bond coverage until the merger is complete and its charter canceled. Depending on the surety bond carrier, the merging credit union may need to provide some documentation to the continuing credit union's carrier before the merger. This documentation may include loan exception workpapers from the most recent examination, copies of previous examination reports, a copy of the most recent supervisory committee audit, and information on recent bond claims.

Required Forms

Within 10 days of the membership vote, the merging federal credit union must notify the NCUA Regional Director of the results (Form NCUA 6308A, 6308B, or 6308C in Appendix A).

The board of directors of both credit unions must execute the merger agreement (Form NCUA 6304 in Appendix A) and submit a copy of the executed agreement to NCUA with the final merger documents at the time the merger is completed. **The effective date of the merger is the date of the executed merger agreement, when the continuing credit union assumes the merging credit union's assets, liabilities, and shares.**

Within 30 days after the effective date of the merger, the continuing credit union must complete the certification of completion of merger (Form NCUA 6309 in Appendix A) and send it to the NCUA Regional Director with the documents with the following attached:

- Financial reports for each credit union immediately before the completion of the merger.
- A consolidated financial report for the continuing credit union immediately after the completion of the merger.
- The charter of the merging federal credit union (if available).
- The insurance certificate for the merging federally insured credit union (if available).
- A copy of the executed merger agreement, Form 6304.

Charter Cancellation

Complete the merger within four months of NCUA approval; otherwise, you must notify the NCUA Regional Director of the reasons for the delay.

We will cancel the merging credit union's charter and/or insurance certificate after we receive all of the required documents, as listed on NCUA Form 6309, Certification of Completion of Merger, in Appendix A.

If the merging credit union's charter isn't canceled by December 31, we will issue an invoice for the applicable NCUSIF operating fee. The continuing credit union will be responsible for paying this invoice.

The continuing credit union is responsible for retaining all documents and records related to the merger.

CHAPTER 2 – CONVERTING TO PRIVATE INSURANCE

STEP 1: PREPARE FOR THE CONVERSION

Permissibility of the Conversion

Part 708b.203 of NCUA's Rules and Regulations describes our procedures and notice requirements for federally-insured, state-chartered credit unions to convert to private insurance if all the following conditions are met:

- State law permits private share insurance.
- Regional Director approves the conversion.
- Affirmative vote of the majority of the credit union's members who vote on the proposition, provided at least 20 percent of the total membership participates in the voting.

Notify NCUA

After your board of directors resolves to seek conversion, you must notify the NCUA Regional Director in writing (Form NCUA IC1 or NCUA IC5 in Appendix B). You are required to provide this written notification to the Regional Director at least 14 days before the credit union notifies its members and seeks their vote and at least 90 days before the proposed conversion date.

STEP 2: CONDUCT THE MEMBERSHIP VOTE

Member Notification

Members have the right to vote on the insurance conversion either at a special meeting or by mail or electronic ballot received no later than the date and time announced for the special meeting. You must provide members with the notice and ballot (Forms NCUA IC2 and NCUA IC3 or Forms NCUA IC6 and NCUA IC7) not more than 30 or less than 7 days before the date of the special meeting. Provide a copy of these documents to the NCUA Regional Director before you mail the notice and ballot to members.

Communicating With Your Members

Federally-insured credit unions must comply with Part 740.2 of NCUA's Rules and Regulations, which prohibits making any representation that is inaccurate or deceptive. Part 708b of NCUA's Rules and Regulations also has the following special requirements for "share insurance communications" (defined in the Glossary on page 18):

1. Every share insurance communication must contain the following conspicuous statement:

IF YOU ARE A MEMBER OF THIS CREDIT UNION, YOUR ACCOUNTS ARE CURRENTLY INSURED BY THE NATIONAL CREDIT UNION ADMINISTRATION, A FEDERAL AGENCY. THIS FEDERAL INSURANCE IS BACKED BY THE FULL FAITH AND CREDIT OF THE UNITED STATES GOVERNMENT. IF THE CREDIT UNION CONVERTS TO PRIVATE INSURANCE AND THE CREDIT UNION FAILS, THE FEDERAL GOVERNMENT DOES NOT GUARANTEE THAT YOU WILL GET YOUR MONEY BACK.

2. You must provide the NCUA Regional Director with a copy of any share insurance communication you intend to make during the voting period. You should provide the copy to the Regional Director before you make it available to members. Along with a copy of the communication, you need to inform the NCUA Regional Director:

- When the communication is to be made,
- To which members it will be directed, and
- How it will be distributed.

The voting period begins on the date the board of directors resolves to seek conversion to private insurance and ends on the date of the membership vote.

Vote Requirements

To ensure the integrity and accuracy of the conversion vote, the vote must be taken by secret ballot. In other words, no credit union employee or official can determine how a particular member voted. In addition, you are required to use an independent entity to collect and tally the votes and certify the results. An independent entity is a company with experience in conducting corporate elections. No official or senior manager of the credit union or their immediate family members may have an ownership interest in, or be employed by, the entity.

STEP 3: COMPLETE THE CONVERSION

Federal Share Insurance Coverage

If your membership and the NCUA Regional Director approve the proposition for conversion of insurance, you are required to give prompt and reasonable notice to the membership. The notice to members must be delivered at least 30 days before the effective date of the conversion. In addition, the notice must identify the effective date of the conversion and the first page must also include a conspicuous statement that:

- The conversion will result in the loss of federal share insurance, and

- The credit union will, at any time before the effective date of conversion, permit all members who have share certificates or other term accounts to close the federally-insured portion of those accounts without an early withdrawal penalty.

Required Certification

Within 10 days of the membership vote, your board of directors and the independent entity that conducts the membership vote must provide NCUA certified results of the vote (Form NCUA IC4 or NCUA IC8 in Appendix B).

Generally, the Regional Director will approve or disapprove the conversion in writing within 14 days of receiving the certification of the vote.

GLOSSARY OF TERMS

Continuing Credit Union: The credit union which will continue in operation after the merger.

Convert, Conversion, Converting: The act of canceling a federal charter and obtaining a state charter or canceling federal share insurance and simultaneously obtaining share or deposit insurance from another insurance carrier, and vice versa.

Effective Date of the Merger: Date of the executed merger agreement, Form NCUA 6304. Also the date when the continuing credit union assumes the merging credit union's assets, liabilities, and shares.

Emergency Merger: A merger in which the merging credit union is insolvent or likely to become insolvent.

Federally insured: Insured by the National Credit Union Administration through the National Credit Union Share Insurance Fund.

Independent Entity: A company with experience in conducting corporate elections. No official or senior manager of the credit union, or the immediate family members of any official or senior manager, may have any ownership interest in, or be employed by, the entity.

Merging Credit Union: The credit union which will cease to exist as an operating credit union at the time of the merger.

Nonfederally insured (privately insured): Insured by a private or cooperative insurance fund or guaranty corporation organized or chartered under state law.

Probable Asset/Share Ratio (PAS): The relative worth of each $1 in shares using an on-going concern concept.

Share Insurance Communication: Any written communication, excluding the forms in Appendix B, made by or on behalf of a federally-insured credit union, intended to be read by two or more credit union members, and that mentions share insurance conversion or termination. The term

- Includes communications delivered or made available before, during, and after the credit union's board of directors decides to seek insurance conversion or termination.
- Includes, but is not limited to, communications delivered or made available by mail, e-mail, and internet website posting.
- Does not include communications intended to be read only by the credit union's own employees or officials.

Supervisory Merger: (For multiple common bond CUs only). A merger in which the merging credit union is experiencing safety and soundness concerns; such as, abandonment of management and/or officials, inability to find replacements, loss of sponsor support, serious and persistent recordkeeping problems, sustained material decline in financial condition, or other serious or persistent circumstances.

Terminate, Termination, and Terminating: The act of canceling federal share insurance. In this case, the credit union's member accounts will become uninsured.

Uninsured: No share or deposit insurance on credit union accounts.

Voluntary Merger: The merger of two financially healthy credit unions.

APPENDIX A - MERGER FORMS

(These forms are designed to be completed electronically. You can download the forms from our web site at www.ncua.gov/

NCUA 6301	Merger Package Checklist
NCUA 6302	Merger Resolution: Continuing Credit Union
NCUA 6303	Merger Resolution: Merging Credit Union
NCUA 6304	Merger Agreement
NCUA 6305A	Notice of Special Meeting of the Members on Proposal to Merge
NCUA 6305B	Notice of Special Meeting on Proposal to Merge and Convert to Nonfederally insured (privately insured) Status
NCUA 6305C	Notice of Special Meeting on Proposal to Merge and Terminate Federal Insurance
NCUA 6306A	Ballot for Merger Proposal
NCUA 6306B	Ballot for Merger Proposal and Conversion to Nonfederally insured (privately insured) Status
NCUA 6306C	Ballot for Merger Proposal and Termination of Federal Insurance
NCUA 6308A	Certification of Vote on Merger Proposal
NCUA 6308B	Certification of Vote on Merger Proposal and Conversion to Nonfederally insured (privately insured) Status
NCUA 6308C	Certification of Vote on Merger Proposal and Termination of Federal Insurance
NCUA 6309	Certification of Completion of Merger
NCUA 6311	Probable Asset/Share Ratio Computation Form (Continuing Credit Union)
NCUA 6312	Probable Asset/Share Ratio Computation Form (Merging Credit Union)

Merger Package Checklist – NCUA 6301

Contents of the Merger Package

- [ ] Detailed explanation of the reason for the merger.

- [ ] Proposed effective date of the merger.

- [ ] Current financial statements for both credit unions.

- [ ] Current delinquent loan summary for both credit unions.

- [ ] Current analysis of the adequacy of the Allowance for Loan and Lease Losses for both credit unions.

- [ ] Consolidated financial statement, including an assessment of the net worth of each credit union before the merger and the net worth of the continuing credit union after the merger.

- [ ] Explanation of any proposed share adjustment.

- [ ] Explanation of any provisions for reserves, undivided earnings, or dividends.

- [ ] Provisions for notifying and paying creditors.

- [ ] Explanation of any changes to insurance, such as life savings and insurance of member accounts.

- [ ] Copies of the merging and continuing credit unions' fields of membership.

- [ ] Information on where the members will be served. The location of the continuing credit union office(s) and/or plans to serve the members through the merging credit union's existing office(s).

- [ ] If the merging credit union has $50 million or more in assets on its latest call report, a statement about whether the two credit unions intend to make a Hart-Scott-Rodino Act premerger notification filing with the Federal Trade Commission and, if not, why not.

- [ ] One primary contact person at both the merging and continuing credit unions and their mailing addresses, e-mail addresses, and phone numbers (for questions or notification of merger decisions).

☐ If the merging credit union is state-chartered and the continuing credit union is federally chartered, evidence that all assets and liabilities meet requirements of the Federal Credit Union Act.

☐ If applicable, evidence your State Supervisory Authority approves of the proposed merger.

☐ If the continuing credit union is nonfederally insured, proof that the accounts of the merging credit union will be accepted for coverage by the nonfederal insurer.

☐ If the continuing credit union is nonfederally insured or uninsured, a written statement from the continuing credit union that it "will fully comply with the requirements of 12.U.S.C. Part 1831t(b), including all notification and acknowledgment requirements."

Required Forms—Federal and State Chartered Credit Unions

☐ NCUA 6302, Merger Resolution: Continuing Credit Union.

☐ NCUA 6303, Merger Resolution: Merging Credit Union.

☐ NCUA 6304, Merger Agreement – submit the proposed merger agreement addressing any share adjustments with the initial application. Submit an executed copy which is signed, dated, and notarized, after the effective date of the merger. Merging and Continuing Credit Unions.

☐ NCUA 6311, Probable Asset/Share Ratio Computation: Continuing Credit Union.

☐ NCUA 6312, Probable Asset/Share Ratio Computation: Merging Credit Union.

Additional Required Forms—Merging Federal Credit Unions

For Federal credit unions merging into a federally insured credit union:

☐ NCUA 6305A, Notice of Special Meeting of the Members on Proposal to Merge.

☐ NCUA 6306A, Ballot for Merger Proposal.

For Federal credit unions merging into a nonfederally insured credit union:

☐ NCUA 6305B, Notice of Special Meeting on Proposal to Merge and Convert to Nonfederally Insured Status.

☐ NCUA 6306B, Ballot for Merger Proposal and Conversion to Nonfederally Insured Status.

For Federal credit unions merging into a credit union with no deposit insurance:

☐ NCUA 6305C, Notice of Special Meeting on Proposal to Merge and Terminate Federal Insurance.

☐ NCUA 6306C, Ballot for Merger Proposal and Termination of Federal Insurance.

Instructions for NCUA 6302: The continuing credit union's board of directors must complete this form after it votes to merge with the merging credit union. This form is required for a complete merger package.

* * * * *

Merger Resolution

Credit Union
(Continuing)

Resolution

The Board of Directors believes our credit union should merge with _____ Credit Union (merging credit union).

Our credit union will assume the merging credit union's shares and liabilities. The merging credit union will transfer to our credit union all of its assets, rights, and property. All members of the merging credit union will receive shares in our credit union, which will stay in business under its present charter.

Certification

We, the Board Presiding Officer and Secretary of this credit union, are authorized to:

- Seek National Credit Union Administration Regional Director approval of the merger.
- Execute and deliver the merger agreement on the effective date of the merger.
- Execute all agreements and other papers required to complete the merger.

We certify to the National Credit Union Administration that the foregoing is a full, true, and correct copy of a resolution adopted by the Board of Directors of our credit union at a meeting held under our bylaws on _____, 20___. A quorum was present and voted. The resolution is duly recorded in the minutes of the meeting and is still in full force and effect.

_____   _____
Board Presiding Officer   Date

_____   _____
Secretary   Date

Instructions for NCUA 6303: The merging credit union's board of directors must complete this form after it votes to merge with the continuing credit union. This form is required for a complete merger package.

* * * * *

Merger Resolution

Credit Union
(Merging)

Resolution

The Board of Directors believes our credit union should merge with   Credit Union (continuing credit union).

The continuing credit union will assume the shares and liabilities of our credit union. Our credit union will transfer to the continuing credit union all of our assets, rights, and property. All members of our credit union will receive shares in the continuing credit union, which will stay in business under its present charter.

Certification

We, the Board Presiding Officer and Secretary of this credit union, are authorized to:

- Seek National Credit Union Administration Regional Director approval of the merger.
- Execute and deliver the merger agreement on the effective date of the merger.
- Execute all agreements and other papers required to complete the merger.

We certify to the National Credit Union Administration that the foregoing is a full, true, and correct copy of a resolution adopted by the Board of Directors of our credit union at a meeting held under our bylaws on   , 20   . A quorum was present and voted. The resolution is duly recorded in the minutes of the meeting and is still in full force and effect.

_____   _____
Board Presiding Officer   Date

_____   _____
Secretary   Date

NCUA 6303 (6/05)

Instructions for NCUA 6304: You must submit a proposed Merger Agreement to the NCUA Regional Director with the initial merger package addressing Item 2, when applicable. Do not sign, date, or notarize the proposed agreement.

At the completion of the merger, officials of the merging and continuing credit unions must complete this agreement, have it notarized, and the continuing credit union should retain the original document. Send one copy of the executed form to the NCUA Regional Director (see Form NCUA 6309). The date you sign this document is the effective date of the merger.

* * * * *

Merger Agreement

This agreement, made and entered into this _____ day of _____, 20 ___, by and between _____ Credit Union (continuing credit union) and _____ Credit Union (merging credit union).

The continuing credit union and the merging credit union agree to the following terms:

1. The merging credit union will transfer to the continuing credit union all of its assets, rights, and property.

2. The continuing credit union will assume and pay all liabilities of the merging credit union. In addition, the continuing credit union will issue all members of the merging credit union the same amount of shares they currently own in the merging credit union, subject to the following share adjustments (if any):

(continuing) Credit Union

by: _____   _____
    Board Presiding Officer   Treasurer

(merging) Credit Union

by: _____   _____
    Board Presiding Officer   Treasurer

NCUA 6304 (6/05)

State of _____

County of _____

Before me a Notary Public (or other authorized officer) appeared the above named and   , Board Presiding Officer and Treasurer of   Credit Union, who being personally known to me as (or proved by the oath of credible witnesses to be) the persons who executed the annexed instrument acknowledged the same to be their free act and deed and in their respective capacities the free act and deed of said credit union.

(SEAL)

Notary Public
My commission expires _____, 20___.

State of _____

County of _____

Before me a Notary Public (or other authorized officer) appeared the above named and   , Board Presiding Officer and Treasurer of   Credit Union,
 who being personally known to me as (or proved by the oath of credible witnesses to be) the persons who executed the annexed instrument acknowledged the same to be their free act and deed and in their respective capacities the free act and deed of said credit union.

(SEAL)

Notary Public
My commission expires _____, 20___.

State of _____

County of _____

NCUA 6304 (6/05)

Instructions for NCUA 6305A: Not more than 30 or less than 7 days before the date of the vote, the merging federal credit union must provide its members (a) advance notice of a special meeting to vote on a proposed merger and (b) a copy of the merger ballot. When you distribute the notice and ballot to your members, you also should send a copy to the NCUA Regional Director. The merging federal credit union should conduct the membership vote only after the NCUA Regional Director approves the proposed merger.

USE THIS FORM ONLY IF THE CONTINUING CREDIT UNION IS FEDERALLY INSURED.

* * * * *

Notice of Special Meeting of the Members on Proposal to Merge

Credit Union
(Merging)

On _____ (insert date), the Board of Directors of your credit union approved a proposition to merge with _____ Credit Union. You are encouraged to attend a special meeting of your credit union at _____ (insert address) on _____, 20____, at _____ (insert date and time).

Purpose of the Meeting

The meeting has two purposes:

1. To consider and act upon a proposal to merge our credit union with _____ Credit Union, the continuing credit union.

2. To approve the action of the Board of Directors of our credit union in authorizing the officers of the credit union, subject to member approval, to carry out the proposed merger.

If this merger is approved, our credit union will transfer all its assets and liabilities to the continuing credit union. As a member of our credit union, you will become a member of the continuing credit union. On the effective date of the merger, you will receive shares in the continuing credit union for the shares you own now in our credit union.

Other Information Related to the Proposed Merger

The directors of the participating credit unions carefully analyzed the assets and liabilities of the participating credit unions and appraised each credit union's share values. The appraisal of the share values appears on the attached individual and consolidated financial statements of the participating credit unions.

The directors of the participating credit unions have concluded that the proposed merger is desirable for the following reasons:

The Board of Directors of our credit union believes that the merger should include/not include an adjustment in shares for the following reasons:

The main office of the continuing credit union will be as follows:

The branch office(s) of the continuing credit union will be as follows:

The merger must have the approval of a majority of members of the credit union who vote on the proposal.

Enclosed with this Notice of Special Meeting is a Ballot for Merger Proposal. If you cannot attend the meeting, please complete the ballot and return it to the credit union office at _____ by no later than _____ on _____, 20____ (insert time and date). To be counted, your ballot must reach us by the date and time announced for the meeting.

BY ORDER OF THE BOARD OF DIRECTORS:

_____   _____
Board Presiding Officer   Date

Instructions for NCUA 6305B: Not more than 30 nor less than 7 days before the date of the vote, the merging federal credit union must provide its members (a) advance notice of a special meeting to vote on a proposed merger and (b) a copy of the merger ballot. When you distribute the notice and ballot to your members, you also should send a copy to the NCUA Regional Director. The merging federal credit union should conduct the membership vote only after the NCUA Regional Director approves the proposed merger.

* * * * *

Notice of Special Meeting on Proposal to Merge and Convert to Nonfederally Insured Status

(insert name of merging credit union)

On _____ (insert date), the Board of Directors of your credit union approved a proposition to merge with _____ (insert name of continuing credit union) and to convert from federal share (deposit) insurance to private insurance. You are encouraged to attend a special meeting of our credit union at _____ (insert address) on _____, 20___, at ___.m. (insert date and time).

Purpose of the Meeting

The meeting has two purposes:

1. To consider and act upon a proposal to merge our credit union with _____ (insert name of continuing credit union), the continuing credit union.

2. To approve the action of the Board of Directors of our credit union in authorizing the officers of the credit union, subject to member approval, to carry out the proposed merger.

If this merger is approved, our credit union will transfer all its assets and liabilities to the continuing credit union. As a member of our credit union, you will become a member of the continuing credit union. On the effective date of the merger, you will receive shares in the continuing credit union for the shares you own in our credit union.

Insurance Conversion

Currently, your accounts have share insurance provided by the National Credit Union Administration, an agency of the federal government. The basic federal coverage is up to $100,000, but accounts may be structured in different ways, such as joint accounts, payable-on-death accounts, or IRA accounts, to achieve federal coverage of much more than $100,000. If the merger is approved, your federal insurance will terminate on the effective date of the merger. Instead, your accounts in the credit union will be insured up to $ (insert dollar amount) by   (insert name of insurer), a corporation chartered by the State of   (insert name of state). The federal insurance provided by the National Credit Union Administration is backed by the full faith and credit of the United States government. The private insurance you will receive from   (insert name of insurer), however, is not guaranteed by the federal or any state or local government.

> **IF THIS MERGER IS APPROVED, AND THE   (insert name of continuing credit union) FAILS, THE FEDERAL GOVERNMENT DOES NOT GUARANTEE YOU WILL GET YOUR MONEY BACK.**

Also, because this merger, if approved, would result in the loss of federal share insurance, the   (insert name of merging credit union) will, at any time between approval of the merger and the effective date of merger and upon request of the member, permit all members who have share certificates or other term accounts to close the federally-insured portion of those accounts without an early withdrawal penalty. (This is an optional sentence. It may be deleted without the approval of the Regional Director. The members must be informed about this right, however, as described in 12 C.F.R. §708b.204(c).)

Other Information Related to the Proposed Merger

The directors of the participating credit unions carefully analyzed the assets and liabilities of the participating credit unions and appraised each credit union's share values. The appraisal of the share values appears on the attached individual and consolidated financial statements of the participating credit unions.

The directors of the participating credit unions have concluded that the proposed merger is desirable for the following reasons:

    (insert reasons)

The Board of Directors of our credit union believes the merger should include/not include an adjustment in shares for the following reasons:

    (insert reasons)

The main office of the continuing credit union will be as follows:

    (insert location)

The branch office(s) of the continuing credit union will be as follows:

    (insert locations)

The merger must have the approval of a majority of members who vote on the proposal, provided at least 20 percent of the total membership participates in the voting.

Enclosed with this Notice of Special Meeting is a Ballot for Merger Proposal and Conversion to Nonfederally Insured Status. If you cannot attend the meeting, please complete the ballot and return it to _____ (insert name of independent entity conducting vote) at _____ (insert mailing address) by no later than _____ on _____, 20__ (insert date and time). To be counted, your ballot must reach _____ (insert name of independent entity conducting vote) by the date and time announced for the meeting.

BY ORDER OF THE BOARD OF DIRECTORS:

_____   _____
Board Presiding Officer   Date
(signature of Board Presiding Officer)

(insert name and title of Board Presiding Officer   (insert date)

Instructions for NCUA 6305C: Not more than 30 or less than 7 days before the date of the vote, the merging federal credit union must provide its members (a) advance notice of a special meeting to vote on a proposed merger and (b) a copy of the merger ballot. When you distribute the notice and ballot to your members, you must also send a copy to the NCUA Regional Director. The merging federal credit union should conduct the membership vote only after the NCUA Regional Director approves the proposed merger.

* * * * *

Notice of Special Meeting on Proposal to Merge and Terminate Federal Insurance

Credit Union
(Merging)

On _____ (insert date), the Board of Directors of your credit union approved a proposition to merge with _____ Credit Union and convert from federal share (deposit) insurance to nonfederal insurance. You are encouraged to attend a special meeting of our credit union at _____ (insert address) on _____, 20___, at _____ (insert date and time).

Purpose of the Meeting

The meeting has two purposes:

1. To consider and act upon a proposal to merge our credit union with _____ Credit Union, the continuing credit union.

2. To approve the action of the Board of Directors of our credit union in authorizing the officers of the credit union to carry out the proposed merger.

If the merger is approved, our credit union will transfer all its assets and liabilities to the continuing credit union. As a member of our credit union, you will become a member of the continuing credit union. On the effective date of the merger, you will receive shares in the continuing credit union for the shares you own now in our credit union.

Insurance Termination

Currently, your accounts have share insurance provided by the National Credit Union Administration, an agency of the federal government. The basic federal coverage is up to $100,000, but accounts may be structured in different ways, such as joint accounts, payable-on-death accounts, or IRA accounts, to achieve federal coverage of much more than $100,000. If the merger is approved, your insurance will be affected as follows:

- After the effective date of the merger, any deposits you make to any new or existing account won't be insured by the National Credit Union Administration or any other entity.
- Your accounts in the merging credit union on the date of the merger, up to a maximum of $100,000 for each member, will remain insured, as provided in the Federal Credit Union Act, for one year after the close of business on the date of the merger.
- If you make any withdrawal after the close of business on the date of the merger, the one-year insurance coverage will be reduced by the amount of the withdrawal.

> **IF THIS MERGER IS APPROVED, AND THE _____ (insert name of continuing credit union) FAILS, THE FEDERAL GOVERNMENT DOES NOT GUARANTEE YOU WILL GET YOUR MONEY BACK.**

The directors of the participating credit unions carefully analyzed the assets and liabilities of the participating credit unions and appraised each credit union's share values. The appraisal of the share values appears on the attached individual and consolidated financial statements of the participating credit unions.

The directors of the participating credit unions have concluded that the proposed merger is desirable for the following reasons:

The Board of Directors of our credit union believes the merger should include/not include an adjustment in shares for the following reasons:

The main office of the continuing credit union will be as follows:

The branch office(s) of the continuing credit union will be as follows:

The merger must have the approval of a majority of our total membership.

Enclosed with this Notice of Special Meeting is a Ballot for Merger Proposal and Termination of Federal Insurance. If you cannot attend the meeting, please complete the ballot and return it to _____ (insert name of the independent entity conducting the vote) at _____ no later than _____, 20___. To be counted, your ballot must reach _____ (insert name of the independent entity) by the date and time announced for the meeting.

BY ORDER OF THE BOARD OF DIRECTORS:

_____   _____
Board Presiding Officer   Date

Instructions for NCUA 6306A: Not more than 30 or less than 7 days before the date of the vote, the merging federal credit union must provide its members (a) advance notice of a special meeting to vote on a proposed merger and (b) a copy of the merger ballot. When you distribute the notice and ballot to your members, you also should send a copy to the NCUA Regional Director. The merging federal credit union should conduct the membership vote only after the NCUA Regional Director approves the proposed merger.

USE THIS FORM ONLY IF THE CONTINUING CREDIT UNION IS FEDERALLY INSURED.

* * * * *

Ballot for Merger Proposal

Name of Member: Account Number:

Your credit union must receive this ballot by _____ (date for vote). Please mail or bring it to:

(insert credit union address)

I have read the Notice of Special Meeting for the members of _____ Credit Union. The meeting will be held on the above date to consider and act upon the merger proposal described in the notice. I vote on the proposal as follows (check one box):

[ ]   **Approve** the proposed merger and authorize the Board of Directors to take all necessary action to accomplish the merger.

[ ]   **Do not approve** the proposed merger.

Signed: _____
            Member's Name

Date: _____

Instructions for NCUA 6306B: Not more than 30 nor less than 7 days before the date of the vote, the merging federal credit union must provide its members (a) advance notice of a special meeting to vote on a proposed merger and (b) a copy of the merger ballot. When you distribute the notice and ballot to your members, you must also send a copy to the NCUA Regional Director.

* * * * *

Ballot for Merger Proposal and Conversion to Nonfederally Insured Status

Name of Member: (insert name) Account Number: (insert account number)

The credit union must receive this ballot by   (insert date and time for vote). Please mail or bring it to:

(insert name of independent entity and address)

I understand if the merger of the   (insert name of merging credit union) into the   (insert name of continuing credit union) is approved, the National Credit Union Administration share (deposit) insurance I now have, up to $100,000, or possibly more if I use different account structures, will terminate upon the effective date of the merger. Instead, my shares in the   (insert name of continuing credit union) will be insured up to $ (insert dollar amount) by   (insert name of insurer), a corporation chartered by the State of   (insert name of state). The federal insurance provided by the National Credit Union Administration is backed by the full faith and credit of the United States Government. The private insurance provided by   (insert name of insurer) is not.

> **I FURTHER UNDERSTAND THAT IF THIS MERGER IS APPROVED, AND THE   (insert name of continuing credit union) FAILS, THE FEDERAL GOVERNMENT DOES NOT GUARANTEE THAT I WILL GET MY MONEY BACK.**

I vote on the proposal as follows (check one box):

[ ] **Approve** merger and conversion to private insurance and authorize the Board of Directors to take all necessary action to accomplish the merger and conversion.

[ ] **Do not approve** merger and conversion to private insurance.

Signed _____ Date:_____
           (insert printed member's name)

NCUA 6306B (6/05)

Instructions for NCUA 6306C: Not more than 30 or less than 7 days before the date of the vote, the merging federal credit union must provide its members (a) advance notice of a special meeting to vote on a proposed merger and (b) a copy of the merger ballot. When you distribute the notice and ballot to your members, you also should send a copy to the NCUA regional director.

* * * * *

Ballot for Merger Proposal and Termination of Federal Insurance

Name of Member: Account Number

We must receive this ballot by   (date for vote). Please mail or bring it to:

(insert name and address of independent entity conducting the vote)

I understand if the merger of the   (merging) Credit Union into the   (continuing) Credit Union is approved, any new deposits or additions to my existing accounts won't be insured by the National Credit Union Administration, an agency of the federal government.

I also understand that my accounts in the continuing credit union on the date of the merger, up to a maximum of $100,000, will be insured for one year after the merger date but that any withdrawals after the merger date will reduce the insurance coverage by the amount of the withdrawal.

> **I FURTHER UNDERSTAND THAT IF THIS MERGER IS APPROVED, AND THE   (insert name of continuing credit union) FAILS, THE FEDERAL GOVERNMENT DOES NOT GUARANTEE THAT I WILL GET MY MONEY BACK EXCEPT AS DESCRIBED ABOVE.**

I vote on the proposal as follows (check one box):

[ ] **Approve** merger and termination of insurance and authorize the Board of Directors to take all necessary action to accomplish the merger and termination.

[ ] **Do not approve** merger and termination of insurance.

Signed _____ Date:_____
          (insert printed member's name)

Instructions for NCUA 6308A: Within 10 days after the membership vote, the merging federal credit union must complete this form and mail it to the NCUA Regional Director.

USE THIS FORM ONLY IF THE CONTINUING CREDIT UNION IS FEDERALLY INSURED.

* * * * *

Certification of Vote on Merger Proposal of the

Credit Union
(Merging)

We, the undersigned officers of the _____ Credit Union, certify the completion of the following actions:

1. At a meeting on _____, 20___, the Board of Directors adopted a resolution approving the merger of our credit union with _____ Credit Union (continuing credit union).

2. Not more than 30 or less than 7 days before the date of the vote, copies of the notice of special meeting and the ballot, as approved by the National Credit Union Administration, and a copy of the merger plan announced in the notice, were mailed to our members.

3. The credit union arranged for a special meeting of our credit union members at the time and place announced in the Notice to consider and act upon the proposed merger.

4. At the special meeting, the credit union arranged for an explanation of the merger proposal and any changes in federally insured status to the members present at the special meeting.

5. Conducted the membership vote at the special meeting. A majority of the voting members of our credit union voted in favor of the merger as follows:
   _____ Number of members present at the special meeting
   _____ Number of members present who voted in favor of the merger
   _____ Number of members present who voted against the merger
   _____ Number of additional written ballots in favor of the merger
   _____ Number of additional written ballots opposed to the merger

6. The action of the members at the special meeting was recorded in the minutes.

This certification signed the   day of   20   .

_____   _____
Board Presiding Officer   Secretary

Instructions for NCUA 6308B: Within 10 days after the membership vote, the merging federal credit union must complete this form and mail it to the NCUA Regional Director.

* * * * *

Certification of Vote on Merger Proposal and Conversion to Nonfederally Insured Status of the Credit Union

(Merging)

We, the undersigned officers of the _____ (insert name of merging credit union), certify the completion of the following actions:

1. At a meeting on (insert date) _____, 20___, the Board of Directors adopted a resolution approving the merger of our credit union with _____ (insert name of continuing credit union).

2. Not more than 30 or less than 7 days before the date of the vote, copies of the notice of special meeting and the ballot, as approved by the National Credit Union Administration, and a copy of the merger plan announced in the notice, were mailed to our members.

3. The credit union arranged for the conduct of a special meeting of our members at the time and place announced in the notice to consider and act upon the proposed merger.

4. At the special meeting, the credit union arranged for an explanation of the merger proposal and any changes in federally insured status to the members present at the special meeting.

5. The _____ (insert name of independent entity), an entity independent of the credit union, conducted the membership vote at the special meeting. At least 20 percent of our total membership voted and a majority of voting members favor the merger as follows:

    (insert) Number of total members
    (insert) Number of members present at the special meeting
    (insert) Number of members present who voted in favor of the merger
    (insert) Number of members present who voted against the merger
    (insert) Number of additional written ballots in favor of the merger
    (insert) Number of additional written ballots opposed to the merger

6. The action of the members at the special meeting was recorded in the minutes.

This certification signed the (insert date) _____ day of _____, 20___.

_____   _____
Board Presiding Officer   Secretary

NCUA 6308B (6/05)

_____   _____
(signature of Board Presiding Officer)   (signature of Board Secretary)
(insert typed name and title)   (insert typed name and title)

I _____ (insert name), an officer of the _____ (insert name of independent entity that conducted the vote), hereby certify that the information recorded in paragraph 5 above is accurate.

This certification signed the (insert date) _____ day of _____, 20___.

_____   _____   _____
Signature   Title   Phone Number
(signature of officer of independent entity)   (typed name, title, and phone number)

NCUA 6308B (6/05)

Instructions for NCUA 6308C: Within 10 days after the membership vote, the merging federal credit union must complete this form and mail it to the NCUA Regional Director.

* * * * *

Certification of Vote on Merger Proposal and Termination of Federal Insurance of the Credit Union

(Merging)

We, the undersigned officers of the _____ Credit Union, certify the completion of the following actions:

1. At a meeting on _____, 20___, the Board of Directors adopted a resolution approving the merger of our credit union with _____ Credit Union (continuing credit union).

2. Not more than 30 or less than 7 days before the date of the vote, copies of the notice of special meeting and the ballot, as approved by the National Credit Union Administration, and a copy of the merger plan announced in the notice, were mailed to our members.

3. The credit union arranged for the conduct of a special meeting of our members at the time and place announced in the notice to consider and act upon the proposed merger.

4. At the special meeting, the credit union arranged for an explanation of the merger proposal and any changes in federally insured status to the members present at the special meeting.

5. The _____ (insert name of independent entity), an entity independent of the credit union, conducted the membership vote at the special meeting. A majority of the members of our credit union voted to approve the merger as follows:
    - _____ Number of total membership
    - _____ Number of members present who voted in favor of the merger
    - _____ Number of members present who voted against the merger
    - _____ Number of additional written ballots in favor of the merger
    - _____ Number of additional written ballots opposed to the merger

6. The action of the members at the special meeting was recorded in the minutes.

This certification signed the _____ day of _____, 20___.

_____   _____
Board Presiding Officer   Secretary

NCUA 6308C (6/05)

I _____ (insert name), an officer of the _____ (insert name of independent entity that conducted the vote), hereby certify that the information recorded in paragraph 5 above is accurate.

This certification signed the _____ day of _____, 20___.

_____   _____   _____
Signature   Title   Phone Number

Instructions for NCUA 6309: Within 30 days after the effective date of the merger, the continuing credit union must complete this form and mail it to the NCUA Regional Director with the documents requested on the form.

* * * * *

Certification of Completion of Merger into Credit Union
(Continuing)

We, the undersigned officers of the above-named credit union, certify to the National Credit Union Administration as follows:

1. The merger of our credit union with _____ Credit Union was completed as of _____, 20___ (date of the executed merger agreement) according to the terms and plan approved by this Board of Directors by a resolution adopted at the meeting held on _____, 20___. We previously provided a certified copy of the resolution to the National Credit Union Administration.

2. We completed all required steps for the merger and transferred the merging credit union's assets.

Attached to this certification are the following documents:

1. Financial reports for each credit union immediately before the completion of the merger.
2. A consolidated financial report for the continuing credit union immediately after the completion of the merger.
3. The charter of the merging federal credit union (if available).
4. The insurance certificate for the merging federally insured credit union (if available).
5. A copy of the executed merger agreement, Form NCUA 6304.

This certification signed the _____ day of _____, 20___.

_____   _____
Board Presiding Officer   Treasurer

NCUA 6309 (6/05)

Instructions for NCUA Forms 6311 and 6312: These probable asset/share ratio computations are required for a complete merger package (not applicable to corporate credit unions).

Probable Asset/Share Ratio Computation Instructions

The Probable Asset/Share Ratio (PAS) reflects the relative worth of $1 of shares in the credit union, assuming it will be an on-going concern. The ratio is computed by dividing the net value of assets by the credit union's total shares.

ADDITIONS:

Cash is valued at book less any known potential losses.

Loans are valued at book net of probable estimated loan losses (ALLL).

Investments are valued at book value less any known losses. However, if a long-term investment is likely to be liquidated prior to maturity, it is valued at current market value.

Fixed Assets are valued at book, except when major fixed assets are not in use or are in the process of being sold. In these instances, the asset is valued at its probable market value.

Other Assets are valued at the most realistic value to the credit union, usually not to exceed book value.

DEDUCTIONS:

Notes Payable are valued at book.

Accounts Payable are valued at book.

Other Liabilities are valued at book.

Contingent and/or Unrecorded Liabilities are valued at the most realistic known value. This item should include any unrecorded dividends not accrued for the accounting period.

Subsidiary Ledger Differences are deducted if the credit union is likely to suffer a loss due to the problem.

Other Losses includes any other known losses. Do not include deficits in undivided earnings or net losses because they have already reduced assets if properly recorded.

PROBABLE ASSET/SHARE RATIO - CONTINUING CREDIT UNION

	Book Value	Market Value
ADDITIONS:		
Cash		
Loans		
Investments		
Fixed Assets		
Other Assets		
Total (A)		$0
DEDUCTIONS:		
Notes Payable		
Accounts Payable		
Other Recorded Liabilities		
Contingent and/or Unrecorded Liabilities		
Subsidiary Ledger Differences (Losses)		
Other Losses		
Total (B)		$0
Net Value of Assets (A-B)		$0
Total Shares		
Probable Asset/Share Ratio		

NCUA6311

PROBABLE ASSET/SHARE RATIO - MERGING CREDIT UNION

	Book Value	Market Value
ADDITIONS:		
Cash		
Loans		
Investments		
Fixed Assets		
Other Assets		
Total (A)		$0
DEDUCTIONS:		
Notes Payable		
Accounts Payable		
Other Recorded Liabilities		
Contingent and/or Unrecorded Liabilities		
Subsidiary Ledger Differences (Losses)		
Other Losses		
Total (B)		$0
Net Value of Assets (A-B)		$0
Total Shares		
Probable Asset/Share Ratio		

NCUA6312

APPENDIX B – INSURANCE CONVERSION FORMS (EXCLUDING MERGERS)

(These forms are designed to be completed electronically. You can download the forms from our web site at www.ncua.gov .)

Federal Charter Converting to Privately-Insured State Charter

NCUA IC1	Notice to NCUA of Intent to Convert and Request for NCUA Approval
NCUA IC2	Notice to Members of Intent to Convert and Member Meeting
NCUA IC3	Member Ballot
NCUA IC4	Certification of Vote

State Charter Converting from Federally-Insured to Privately-Insured

NCUA IC5	Notice to NCUA of Intent to Convert and Request for NCUA Approval
NCUA IC6	Notice to Members of Intent to Convert and Member Meeting
NCUA IC7	Member Ballot
NCUA IC8	Certification of Vote

Notice to NCUA of Intent to Convert to State Charter and to Nonfederal (Private) Share Insurance and Request for NCUA Approval

Instructions for NCUA IC1: The converting credit union must provide this letter to the NCUA Regional Director at least 14 days before the credit union notifies its members of the proposed conversion and solicits their vote on the conversion and at least 90 days before the proposed conversion date.

* * * * *

(insert name), NCUA Regional Director

(insert address of NCUA Regional Director)

Re: Notice of Intent to Convert to State Charter and Private Share Insurance

Dear Director   (insert name):

In accordance with federal law at Title 12, United States Code Section 1785(b)(1)(D), I request the National Credit Union Administration approve the conversion of   (insert name of federal credit union) to a state charter in   (insert name of state) and from federal share insurance to private primary share insurance with   (insert name of private insurance company).

On   (insert date), the board of directors of   (insert name of credit union) resolved to pursue the charter conversion and the conversion from federal insurance to private insurance. A copy of the resolution is enclosed.

On   (insert date), the credit union plans to solicit the vote of our members on the conversion. The credit union will employ   (insert name, address, and telephone number of independent entity) to conduct the vote. The credit union will use the form notice and ballot required by NCUA regulations, and will certify the results to NCUA as required by NCUA regulations.

Aside from the notice and ballot, the credit union (does)(does not) intend to provide our members with additional written information about the conversion. I understand that NCUA regulations forbid any communications to members, including communications about NCUA insurance or private insurance, that are inaccurate or deceptive.

I have enclosed a copy of a letter from   (insert name and title of state regulator) indicating approval of our conversion to a state charter.

(Insert name of state) allows credit unions to obtain primary share insurance from   (insert name of private insurance company). I have enclosed a copy of a letter from   (insert name and title of state regulator) establishing that   (insert name of private insurer) has the authority to provide   (insert name of credit union), after conversion to a state charter, with primary share insurance.

I have enclosed a copy of a letter from _____ (insert name of private insurer) indicating it has accepted _____ (insert name of credit union) for primary share insurance and will insure the credit union immediately upon the date that it loses its federal share insurance.

I am aware of the requirements of 12 U.S.C. §1831t(b), including all notification and acknowledgment requirements.

Enclosed you will also find other information required by NCUA's Chartering and Field of Membership Manual, Chapter 4, §III.C.

The point of contact for conversion matters is _____ (insert name and title of credit union employee), who can be reached at _____ (insert telephone number).

                                        Sincerely,

                                        (signature)

                                        Chief Executive Officer

Enclosures

Instructions for NCUA IC2: The converting federal credit union must notify its members of a special meeting to vote on the conversion and provide its members a copy of the conversion ballot. The notice and ballot must be given to members (a) at least 14 days after the credit union notifies NCUA of its intent to convert and (b) not more than 30 nor less than 7 days before the date of the special meeting. When the converting credit union distributes this notice to its members it should also send a copy to the NCUA Regional Director, if it has not already done so.

* * * * *

Notice of Proposal to Convert to a State Charter and to Nonfederally Insured Status and Special Meeting of Members

(insert name of converting credit union)

On   (insert date), the board of directors of your credit union approved a proposition to convert from federal share (deposit) insurance to private insurance and to convert from a federal credit union to a state-chartered credit union. You are encouraged to attend a special meeting of our credit union at   (insert address) on   , 20   , at (insert date and time) to address this proposition.

Purpose of Meeting
The meeting has two purposes:

1. To consider and act upon a proposal to convert your credit union from a federal charter to a state charter and your account insurance from federal insurance to private insurance.
2. To approve the action of the Board of Directors in authorizing the officers of the credit union to carry out the proposed conversion.

Insurance Conversion
Currently, your accounts have share insurance provided by the National Credit Union Administration, an agency of the federal government. The basic federal coverage is up to $100,000, but accounts may be structured in different ways, such as joint accounts, payable-on-death accounts, or IRA accounts, to achieve federal coverage of much more than $100,000. If the conversion is approved, your federal insurance will terminate on the effective date of the conversion. Instead, your accounts in the credit union will be insured up to $ (insert dollar amount) by   (insert name of insurer), a corporation chartered by the State of   (insert name of state). The federal insurance provided by the National Credit Union Administration is backed by the full faith and credit of the United States government. The private insurance you will receive from   (insert name of insurer), however, is not guaranteed by the federal or any state or local government.

IF THIS CONVERSION IS APPROVED, AND THE (insert name of credit union) FAILS, THE FEDERAL GOVERNMENT DOES NOT GUARANTEE YOU WILL GET YOUR MONEY BACK.

Also, because this conversion, if approved, would result in the loss of federal share insurance, the credit union will, at any time between the approval of the conversion and the effective date of conversion and upon request of the member, permit all members who have share certificates or other term accounts to close the federally-insured portion of those accounts without an early withdrawal penalty. (This is an optional sentence. It may be deleted without the approval of the Regional Director. The members must be informed about this right, however, as described in 12 C.F.R. §708b.204(c).)

The board of directors has concluded that the proposed conversion is desirable for the following reasons: (This is an optional paragraph. It may be deleted without the prior approval of the Regional Director.)

The proposed conversion will result in the following one-time costs associated with the conversion: (List the total estimated dollar amount, including (1) the cost of conducting the vote, (2) the cost of changing the credit union's name and insurance logo, and (3) attorney and consultant fees.)

The conversion must have the approval of a majority of members who vote on the proposal, provided at least 20 percent of the total membership participates in the voting.

Enclosed with this Notice of Special Meeting is a ballot. If you cannot attend the meeting, please complete the ballot and return it to   (insert name and address of independent entity conducting the vote) by no later than   on   , 20   (insert time and date). To be counted, your ballot must reach us by that date and time.

BY ORDER OF THE BOARD OF DIRECTORS:

_____   _____
Board Presiding Officer   Date

(insert title)

Instructions for NCUA IC3: The converting federal credit union must notify its members of a special meeting to vote on the conversion and provide its members a copy of the conversion ballot. The notice and ballot must be given to members (a) at least 14 days after the credit union notifies the NCUA Regional Director of its intent to convert and (b) not more than 30 nor less than 7 days before the date of the special meeting. When the converting credit union distributes this notice to its members it should also send a copy to the NCUA Regional Director, if it has not already done so.

* * * * *

Ballot for Conversion to State Charter and Nonfederally Insured Status

(<u>insert name of converting credit union</u>)

Name of Member: (insert name) Account Number: (insert account number)

The credit union must receive this ballot by   (insert date and time for vote). Please mail or bring it to:

(Insert name of independent entity and address)

I understand if the conversion of   (insert name of credit union) is approved, the National Credit Union Administration share (deposit) insurance I now have, up to $100,000, or possibly more if I use different account structures, will terminate upon the effective date of the conversion. Instead, my shares in the   (insert name of credit union) will be insured up to $ (insert dollar amount) by   (insert name of insurer), a corporation chartered by the State of   (insert name of state). The federal insurance provided by the National Credit Union Administration is backed by the full faith and credit of the United States Government. The private insurance provided by   (insert name of insurer) is not.

I FURTHER UNDERSTAND THAT IF THIS CONVERSION IS APPROVED, AND THE   (insert name of credit union) FAILS, THE FEDERAL GOVERNMENT DOES NOT GUARANTEE THAT I WILL GET MY MONEY BACK.

I vote on the proposal as follows (check one box):

[ ] **Approve** the conversion of charter and conversion to private insurance and authorize the Board of Directors to take all necessary action to accomplish the conversion.

[ ] **Do not approve** the conversion of charter and the conversion to private insurance.

Signed _____ Date_____
         (insert printed member's name)

Instructions for NCUA IC4: Within 10 days after the membership vote, the converting credit union must complete this form and mail it to the NCUA Regional Director.

* * * * *

Certification of Vote on Conversion to State Charter and Nonfederally Insured Status

We, the undersigned officers of the _____ (insert name of converting credit union), certify the completion of the following actions:

1. At a meeting on _____ (insert date), the Board of Directors adopted a resolution to seek the conversion of our credit union to a state charter and the conversion of our primary share insurance coverage from NCUA to _____ (insert name of private insurer).

2. Not more than 30 or less than 7 days before the date of the vote, copies of the notice of special meeting and ballot, as approved by the NCUA, were mailed to our members.

3. The credit union arranged for the conduct of a special meeting of our members at the time and place announced in the Notice to consider and act upon the proposed conversion.

4. At the special meeting, the credit union arranged for an explanation of the conversion to the members present at the special meeting.

5. The _____ (insert name), an entity independent of the credit union, conducted the membership vote at the special meeting. The members voted as follows:
   (insert) Number of total members
   (insert) Number of members present at the special meeting
   (insert) Number of members present who voted in favor of the conversion
   (insert) Number of members present who voted against the conversion
   (insert) Number of additional written ballots in favor of the conversion
   (insert) Number of additional written ballots opposed to the conversion

   (Insert "20% or more") **OR** (Insert "Less than 20%") of the total membership voted. Of those who voted, a majority voted (Insert "in favor of") **OR** (Insert "against") conversion.

The action of the members at the special meeting was recorded in the minutes.

This certification signed the (insert date) _____ day of _____, 20__.

_____   _____
Board Presiding Officer   Secretary
(insert typed name and title)   (insert typed name and title_)

I   (insert name), an officer of the   (insert name of independent entity that conducted the vote), hereby certify that the information recorded in paragraph 5 above is accurate.

This certification signed the(insert date) _____ day of _____, 20__.

_____   _____   _____
Signature   Title   Phone Number

(insert signature of officer of independent entity) (insert typed name, title, and phone number)

Notice to NCUA of Intent to Convert to Nonfederal (Private) Share Insurance and Request for NCUA Approval

Instructions for NCUA IC5: The converting state chartered credit union must provide this letter to the NCUA Regional Director at least 14 days before the credit union notifies its members of the proposed conversion and solicits their vote on the conversion and at least 90 days before the proposed conversion date.

* * * * *

(insert name), NCUA Regional Director

(insert address of NCUA Regional Director)

Re: Notice of Intent to Convert to Private Share Insurance

Dear Director   (insert name):

In accordance with federal law at Title 12, United States Code Section 1785(b)(1)(D), I request the National Credit Union Administration approve the conversion of (insert name of credit union) from federal share insurance to private primary share insurance with   (insert name of private insurance company).

On   (insert date), the board of directors of   (insert name of credit union) resolved to pursue the conversion from federal insurance to private insurance. A copy of the resolution is enclosed.

On   (insert date), the credit union plans to solicit the vote of our members on the conversion. The credit union will employ   (insert name, address, and telephone number of independent entity) to conduct the member vote. The credit union will use the form notice and ballot required by NCUA regulations, and will certify the results to NCUA as required by NCUA regulations.

Aside from the notice and ballot, the credit union (does)(does not) intend to provide its members with additional written information about the conversion. I understand that NCUA regulations forbid any communications to members, including communications about NCUA insurance or private insurance, that are inaccurate or deceptive.

(Insert name of state) allows credit unions to obtain primary share insurance from   (insert name of private insurance company). I have enclosed a copy of a letter from   (insert name and title of state regulator) establishing that   (insert name of private insurer) has the authority to provide   (insert name of credit union) with primary share insurance.

I have enclosed a copy of a letter from   (insert name of private insurer) indicating it has accepted   (insert name of credit union) for primary share insurance and will insure the credit union immediately upon the date that it loses its federal share insurance.

I am aware of the requirements of 12 U.S.C. §1831t(b), including all notification and acknowledgment requirements.

The point of contact for conversion matters is _____ (insert name and title of credit union employee), who can be reached at _____ (insert telephone number).

                              Sincerely,

                              (signature)
                              Chief Executive Officer

Enclosures

Instructions for NCUA IC6: The converting state-chartered credit union must notify its members of a special meeting to vote on the conversion and provide its members a copy of the conversion ballot. The notice and ballot must be given to members (a) at least 14 days after the credit union notifies the NCUA Regional Director of its intent to convert and (b) not more than 30 nor less than 7 days before the date of the special meeting. When the converting credit union distributes this notice to its members it should also send a copy to the NCUA Regional Director, if it has not already done so.

* * * * *

Notice of Proposal to Convert to Nonfederally Insured Status and Special Meeting of Members

(insert name of converting credit union)

On   (insert date), the board of directors of your credit union approved a proposition to convert from federal share (deposit) insurance to private insurance. You are encouraged to attend a special meeting of our credit union at   (insert address) on   , (insert time and date) to address this proposition.

Purpose of Meeting

The meeting has two purposes:

1. To consider and act upon a proposal to convert your account insurance from federal insurance to private insurance.

2. To approve the action of the Board of Directors in authorizing the officers of the credit union to carry out the proposed conversion.

Insurance Conversion

Currently, your accounts have share insurance provided by the National Credit Union Administration, an agency of the Federal Government. The basic federal coverage is up to $100,000, but accounts may be structured in different ways, such as joint accounts, payable-on-death accounts, or IRA accounts, to achieve federal coverage of much more than $100,000. If the conversion is approved, your federal insurance will terminate on the effective date of the conversion. Instead, your accounts in the continuing credit union will be insured up to $ (insert dollar amount) by   (insert name of insurer), a corporation chartered by the State of   (insert name of the state). The federal insurance provided by the National Credit Union Administration is backed by the full faith and credit of the United States government. The private insurance you will receive from   (insert name of insurer) is not guaranteed by the federal or any state or local government.

> **IF THIS CONVERSION IS APPROVED, AND THE ____ (insert name of credit union) FAILS, THE FEDERAL GOVERNMENT DOES NOT GUARANTEE YOU WILL GET YOUR MONEY BACK.**

Also, because this conversion, if approved, would result in the loss of federal share insurance, the credit union will, at any time between the approval of the conversion and the effective date of conversion and upon request by the member, permit all members who have share certificates or other term accounts to close the federally-insured portion of those accounts without an early withdrawal penalty. (This is an optional sentence. It may be deleted without the approval of the Regional Director. The members must be informed about this right, however, as described in 12 C.F.R. §708b.204(c).)

The board of directors has concluded that the proposed conversion is desirable for the following reasons: (insert reasons) (This is an optional paragraph. It may be deleted without the prior approval of the Regional Director.)

The proposed conversion will result in the following one-time costs associated with the conversion (List the total estimated dollar amount, including (1) the cost of conducting the vote, (2) the cost of changing the credit union's name and insurance logo, and (3) attorney and consultant fees.)

The conversion must have the approval of a majority of members who vote on the proposal, provided at least 20 percent of the total membership participates in the voting.

Enclosed with this Notice of Special Meeting is a ballot. If you cannot attend the meeting, please complete the ballot and return it to ____ (insert name and address of independent entity conducting the vote) by no later than ____ (insert time and date). To be counted, your ballot must reach us by that date and time.

BY ORDER OF THE BOARD OF DIRECTORS:

_____   _____
Board Presiding Officer   Date
(insert title)

Instructions for NCUA IC7: The converting state-chartered credit union must notify its members of a special meeting to vote on the conversion and provide its members a copy of the conversion ballot. The notice and ballot must be given to members (a) at least 14 days after the credit union notifies NCUA of its intent to convert and (b) not more than 30 nor less than 7 days before the date of the special meeting. When the converting credit union distributes this notice to its members it should also send a copy to the NCUA Regional Director, if it has not already done so.

* * * * *

Ballot for Conversion to Nonfederally Insured Status

(<u>insert name of converting credit union</u>)

Name of Member: (insert name)   Account Number: (insert account number)

The credit union must receive this ballot by   (insert date and time for vote). Please mail or bring it to: (Insert name and address of independent entity and address)

I understand if the conversion of the   (insert name of credit union) is approved, the National Credit Union Administration share (deposit) insurance I now have, up to $100,000, or possibly more if I use different account structures, will terminate upon the effective date of the conversion. Instead, my shares in the   (insert name of credit union) will be insured up to $ (insert dollar amount) by   (insert name of insurer), a corporation chartered by the State of   (insert name of state). The federal insurance provided by the National Credit Union Administration is backed by the full faith and credit of the United States Government. The private insurance provided by   (insert name of insurer) is not.

> **I FURTHER UNDERSTAND THAT IF THIS CONVERSION IS APPROVED, AND THE   (insert name of credit union) FAILS, THE FEDERAL GOVERNMENT DOES NOT GUARANTEE THAT I WILL GET MY MONEY BACK.**

I vote on the proposal as follows (check one box):

[ ] **Approve** the conversion to private insurance and authorize the Board of Directors to take all necessary action to accomplish the conversion.

[ ] **Do not approve** the conversion to private insurance.

Signed _____   Date_____
       (insert printed member's name)

Instructions for NCUA IC8: Within 10 days after the membership vote, the converting credit union must complete this form and mail it to the NCUA Regional Director.

* * * * *

Certification of Vote on Conversion to Nonfederally Insured Status

We, the undersigned officers of the _____ (insert name of converting credit union), certify the completion of the following actions:

1. At a meeting on _____ (insert date), the Board of Directors adopted a resolution to seek the conversion of our primary share insurance coverage from NCUA to _____ (insert name of private insurer).

2. Not more than 30 or less than 7 days before the date of the vote, copies of the notice of special meeting and the ballot, as approved by the National Credit Union Administration, were mailed to our members.

3. The credit union arranged for the conduct of a special meeting of our members at the time and place announced in the Notice to consider and act upon the proposed conversion.

4. At the special meeting, the credit union arranged for an explanation of the conversion to the members present at the special meeting.

5. The _____ (Insert name), an entity independent of the credit union, conducted the membership vote at the special meeting. The members voted as follows:
   (insert) Number of total members
   (insert) Number of members present at the special meeting
   (insert) Number of members present who voted in favor of the conversion
   (insert) Number of members present who voted against the conversion
   (insert) Number of additional written ballots in favor of the conversion
   (insert) Number of additional written ballots opposed to the conversion

   (Insert "20% or more") **OR** (Insert "Less than 20%") of the total membership voted. Of those who voted, a majority voted (Insert "in favor of") **OR** (Insert "against") conversion.

The action of the members at the special meeting was recorded in the minutes.

This certification signed the _____ day of _____, 20__.

_____   _____
Board Presiding Officer   Secretary
(insert typed name and title)   (insert typed name and title)

I _____ (insert name), an officer of the _____ (insert name of independent entity that conducted the vote), hereby certify that the information recorded in paragraph 5 above is accurate.

This certification signed the _____ day of _____, 20__.

(signature of officer of independent entity)(typed name, title, and phone number)

www.ingramcontent.com/pod-product-compliance
Lightning Source LLC
Chambersburg PA
CBHW062121220526
45471CB00010B/3831